Everything
You Need to
Know About

AIDS
and HIV

Scheduling an HIV test is an important part of your overall health care.

Everything You Need to Know About AIDS and HIV

Katherine White

The Rosen Publishing Group, Inc.
New York

Published in 2001 by The Rosen Publishing Group, Inc.
29 East 21st Street, New York, NY 10010

Copyright © 2001 by The Rosen Publishing Group, Inc.

First Edition

Library of Congress Cataloging-in-Publication Data

White, Katherine (Katherine G.)
Everything you need to know about AIDS and HIV/by Katherine White.—1st ed.
p.; cm. — (The need to know library)
Includes bibliographical references and index.
ISBN 0-8239-3314-8
1. AIDS (Disease)—Juvenile literature. [1. AIDS (Disease) 2. HIV (Viruses) 3. Diseases.] [DNLM: 1. HIV Infections—Popular Works. WC 503 W585k 2001] I. Title. II. Series.
RC606.65 .W475 2001
616.97'92—dc21

                                                  2001001273

Manufactured in the United States of America

Contents

Introduction   6

Chapter 1   Discovery and
     Definition   8

Chapter 2   Contracting the Virus   19

Chapter 3   Getting Tested   29

Chapter 4   Living with HIV
     and AIDS   41

Glossary   55

Where to Go for Help   57

For Further Reading   60

Index   62

Introduction

If you were to ask someone—a parent, friend, teacher, or sibling—what AIDS is, it is more than likely he or she would not only recognize the name of the disease, but would also be able to tell you about it. You probably know something about AIDS (acquired immunodeficiency syndrome) and HIV (human immunodeficiency virus), too. AIDS is one of the greatest challenges faced by the population of the world today. As of the year 2000, over 35 million people worldwide have been infected with the HIV virus. That's a large chunk of the population, and sadly, each year more and more people are becoming infected. This means that you, as an individual, need to know what to do to protect yourself.

Taking proper precautions to prevent infection is one of the most important steps toward combating this disease, especially because it affects such a significant portion of people in the United States and the rest of the world. It is also crucial that you understand the origin of the disease, what it is, and how it affects your body, particularly your immune system. And, since many people who are infected with the HIV virus are leading longer, healthier lives, it is essential to extinguish the misinformation that surrounds the illness and those who are sick with it.

In this book, you will learn the ins and outs of both HIV and AIDS. Both the virus and the disease will be explained to you, from how a person first contracts the HIV virus to the development of full-blown AIDS. Again, how you can protect yourself from contracting, or getting, the HIV virus will be discussed, as will new treatments and research. Although the road to this disease's extinction is a long one, scientists and researchers are working exceptionally hard to attain that goal. As the fight continues, education about AIDS and HIV is vital.

Chapter 1

Discovery and Definition

On June 4, 1981 in a weekly newsletter put out by the Centers for Disease Control and Prevention (CDC), the arrival of AIDS was shared with the public for the first time. It was a quiet announcement, not read by many people. At the time, reports came in solely from the Los Angeles area, where the immune systems of five homosexual men no longer prevented infections that should have been easy for their bodies to fight off. Each man suffered from a cancer called Kaposi's sarcoma, and the disease was labeled "gay cancer." (It was later referred to as gay-related immune deficiency, or GRID). However, by the end of the year doctors from many major cities in Texas, New York, and Florida reported similar cases.

The stories were all the same. People who were otherwise considered very healthy became sick with illnesses that their previously healthy bodies should have subdued. It was soon discovered that this illness did not affect gay men exclusively. People who shared needles during intravenous drug use (drugs injected into the bloodstream using a needle) and hemophiliacs were becoming infected, too. Hemophilia is a condition in which normal blood clotting does not occur, so the person bleeds profusely. Whereas a healthy person might scrape a knee and bleed only enough blood to fill a bandage, a hemophiliac might lose so much blood that he or she needs to be hospitalized and undergo a blood transfusion.

A Shared Trait

In 1982, the CDC linked this mysterious disease to the blood. From that point on, researchers referred to the disease by its current name, AIDS. This breakthrough also led to the identification of each infected person's common trait. Every patient lacked white blood cells; specifically, they were missing what are called T-helper cells. White blood cells, the T-helper cells in particular, are the cells in your body that make up and keep your immune system functioning properly. Your immune system is the body system in charge of fighting off infection. It keeps you free of all types of illness, from the common cold to pneumonia.

During these first few years, a person was diagnosed with AIDS only as a result of encountering his or her first serious health problem. Most people died only a year or two after the diagnosis. But in 1983, the medical field

AIDS: The Early Years

◎ 1981: AIDS is first reported; at the time, it is called GRID.

422 cases are diagnosed in the United States; 159 people die

◎ 1982: The term "AIDS" is first used.

1,614 cases diagnosed, 619 people die

◎ 1983: Institut Pasteur identifies HIV.

4,740 cases diagnosed, 2,122 people die

◎ 1984: President Ronald Reagan has not yet said the word "AIDS" in public.

11,055 cases diagnosed, 5,620 people die

made a major leap that provided a greater understanding of what the medical community and the population faced. The outlook was not very good.

Discovery of HIV

In 1983, the Institut Pasteur in France established that HIV was the virus that caused AIDS, and as a result, some of the most basic questions about the disease

- 1985: The Food and Drug Administration (FDA) approves the first HIV test.

  22,996 cases diagnosed, 12,592 people die

- 1986: A report on AIDS is written by Surgeon General C. Everett Koop.

  42,255 cases diagnosed, 24,669 people die

- 1987: AZT, the first treatment for AIDS, is approved by the FDA.

  71,176 cases diagnosed, 41,027 people die

- 1988: FDA decides to make new therapies available sooner to people who suffer from disease, specifically AIDS.

  106,994 cases diagnosed, 62,101 people die

were answered. Researchers now understood that the virus passed from one person to another: through sexual contact—sharing body fluids, like semen—or by coming into contact with an infected person's blood. Bear in mind that at this point, knowledge about the disease, though helpful, was still very limited.

Two years later, in 1985, researchers announced another medical achievement. People could now be tested for the HIV virus with a blood test. This meant that not only could people find out if they were infected, but also that doctors could begin to study the disease more closely.

While a person with full-blown AIDS looked and felt sick, HIV did not present any symptoms. A person did not feel weak or tired, nor did he or she become sick more easily. In fact, a person might not have symptoms for a few years, but once infected, he or she could unknowingly infect others. For every person who was sick with AIDS, thousands were infected with the HIV virus. As reported in the article "Epidemic: An Overview" in the *New York Times*, "at the end of 1988 almost 90,000 Americans had been diagnosed with AIDS, and almost 50,000 had died of the illness. But public health officials were estimating that close to a million might be carrying the virus."

What Are AIDS and HIV?

Discussing HIV and AIDS can be painful, as this disease has taken the lives of many people. For example, it was not until mid-1985 that doctors and scientists began to test blood being used in blood transfusions for HIV. This means that anyone who received blood between the years 1978 and 1985 could have been infected with the HIV virus. Sadly, in this way, many hemophiliacs were accidentally infected and later died. But what is it about AIDS that makes it so deadly? And why is it that a person can live with HIV for years without knowing it?

Once the AIDS epidemic spread beyond the gay community, the mainstream press finally took the deadly disease seriously.

Origin of AIDS

For many years, scientists and researchers have focused on determining when AIDS came into being; its genesis. After many years of research, the exact date remains unclear. The latest theory, developed in February 2000, claims that the HIV virus came into being sometime between 1910 and 1950, though 1930 seems the most likely date. Regardless of the exact date, most AIDS researchers now agree as to how the disease came to infect humans. It is believed that a relative of the chimpanzee carried the virus and that it eventually, through contact, infected the human race.

Human Immunodeficiency Virus

The body's immune system contains more than 100 million immune cells. These cells, which make up the organs of the immune system, such as the spleen and adenoids, work hard to destroy any infections that invade the body. When a virus or bacteria enters the body, certain immune cells are designed to hunt it down and fight it off. In the case of human

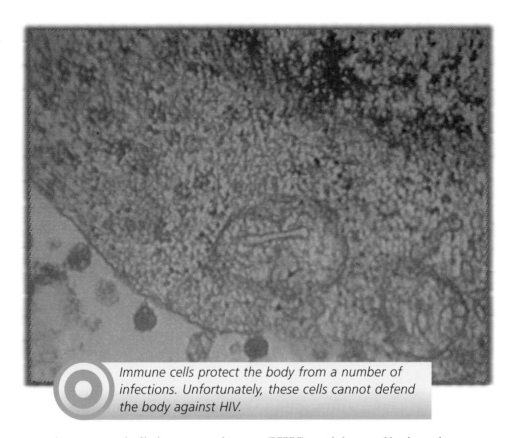

Immune cells protect the body from a number of infections. Unfortunately, these cells cannot defend the body against HIV.

immunodeficiency virus (HIV), this cell is the T-helper cell. When a person is infected with the HIV virus, the immune system dispatches a large number of T-helper cells to destroy it. However, T-helper cells cannot fight off HIV; instead, the virus not only infects the cells, but eventually kills them. So HIV weakens the immune system by directly attacking it, though neither AIDS nor HIV actually kills an infected person.

Whereas a healthy immune system has between 500 and 1800 T-helper cells, a person who has HIV will steadily lose that number. As a result, a large part of his or her immune system is no longer there

A Closer Look: Inside a Cell

T-cell Infection: The HIV virus enters the body and T-helper cells are sent to fight it. Instead, though, the virus attaches itself to a protein on the cell called the CD4. This causes the virus to fuse with the T-helper cell, letting the virus get inside of the cell.

Replication: Now that the virus is in the cell, it can use parts of the T-helper cell to copy itself. It copies itself thousands of times within the T-helper cell and then it rises to the surface of the cell.

Release: Once at the surface of the cell, a portion of the cell called the cell membrane turns itself inside out, and new viruses leave the cell.

Cell Death: These new infected cells can now go find other healthy cells and repeat the process, until no healthy T-helper cells exist.

to help fight off diseases. The person is left without enough defenses to ward off illnesses that would normally be easy to beat. Most people who die of AIDS die from tuberculosis, cancer, lung disease, or other infections.

Why Is HIV Hard to Recognize?

If all this stuff is happening inside of someone's body you would think that he or she would know it, right? However, this is not so. The rate at which the HIV virus infects the T-helper cells is different in every person. Even now, after years of study, scientists still do not know why the virus destroys some people's T-helper cells more slowly than others'.

But what does that mean? Let's say a person has become infected with HIV, but for whatever reason he or she does not lose the number of T-helper cells required to make a person feel sick. In fact, a person may not feel any signs of HIV for five years. Although a person who has HIV can lead a rather healthy life, he or she does have to take precautions so as not to infect other people. If a person does not know about the infection, he or she will most likely not take care to shield others from the disease. Therefore, he or she may infect other people with the virus.

What Is AIDS?

All this talk about HIV and the fact that a person is not immediately diagnosed with AIDS can be confusing. AIDS is the disease that a person with HIV develops once his or her T-helper cell count drops below 200. However, doctors also diagnose a person with AIDS if he or she has other sicknesses, such as tuberculosis or pneumonia, even if his or her cell count is above 200. In other words, the HIV virus is what kills off the cells of the immune system. But, once the immune system is weakened to a certain point (below 200 T-helper cells), the person has the disease AIDS.

Since 1991, AIDS has been the sixth leading cause of death among fifteen- to twenty-four-year-olds, and one in five people newly diagnosed with AIDS is twenty to twenty-nine years old. This is why the next chapter will focus on how a person contracts the virus; if you know how to protect yourself, you will be able to stay healthy.

Chapter 2

Contracting the Virus

Contracting HIV and AIDS is a very real possibility for teens, and it should be one of your major concerns. But for so many teens, it seems like a distant reality, something that could never happen to them. Consequently, few take the precautions that they should. Also, many myths persist as to how a person contracts the disease. In order to take control of your life, to live healthy and stay that way, it is especially important that you not only know the facts about AIDS but also act accordingly.

Overall, there are three ways in which a person can contract the HIV virus:

◎ Sharing sexual fluids

◎ Coming in contact with an infected person's blood

◎ An infected mother passing the disease to her unborn baby

Issues of Sex

The phrase "sharing sexual fluids" means engaging in sex. For example, if a woman has intercourse with a man who has HIV, without a condom, she could become infected. Any tiny cut or sore inside of her vagina could make it easy for the virus to pass into her body. Conversely, if an infected woman has intercourse with a man without a condom, the virus could enter the man's bloodstream through a sore spot, or through the tube that runs down the length of the penis. Unfortunately, sore spots or cuts are usually so small that they may not be seen or felt. The virus may also be transmitted in same-sex relationships when bodily fluids are shared.

Is Safe Sex Possible?

Practicing safe sex is always important, but in order to avoid the spread of HIV, it is crucial. Kissing, hand-holding, massaging, and rubbing bodies are all completely safe sexual practices. In fact, there is no way that you can become infected with the HIV virus if you limit yourself to these practices.

There are many ways to show affection and practice safe sex.

For many reasons, it is important to use a condom to protect you and your partner.

Oral sex is almost absolutely safe, because it is rare that a person becomes infected with HIV from having it. However, it can happen, so there is some risk of infection. Whereas with intercourse, an open sore on the genitalia allows the infection to spread, with oral sex an open sore in the mouth can put a person at risk. Because fluids are released from one partner into the the other partner's mouth, the possibility of infection exists.

Finally then, how safe is sex? Abstinence, or not having sex, is the only foolproof method of preventing the spread of HIV or AIDS. But if you are going to have sex, be smart. Having sex with a condom is a

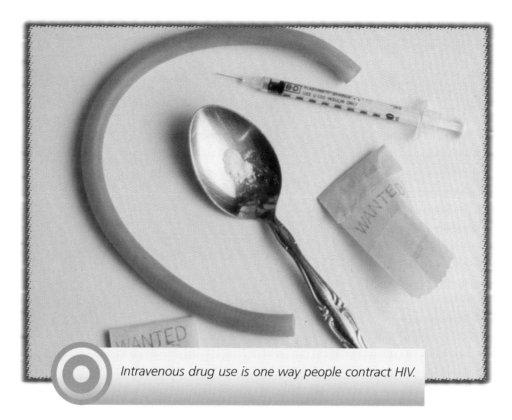

Intravenous drug use is one way people contract HIV.

must and usually keeps you safe. The operative word is "usually." Condoms have a tendency to break, and when they do, the chance of infection due to the sharing of bodily fluids increases.

Contact with Blood

Coming into direct contact with the blood of a person who has been infected with HIV also poses a threat. When researchers figured out how AIDS was contracted, the medical profession got quite a scare. Doctors, nurses, dentists, emergency medical technicians (EMTs), and surgeons come in contact with many patients on a daily basis. With the discovery of HIV and increased knowledge about how it was transmitted, medical professionals realized they needed to protect themselves. Now, not only do medical professionals wear latex gloves when dealing with all patients, they also use a safety device when administering mouth-to-mouth resuscitation.

For most teens, though, the threat of infection comes from intravenous drug use and from having sex without a condom. When sharing needles, little droplets of blood are caught in the dispenser part of the needle. If another person fills up the syringe with drugs and then injects him or herself, he or she is coming in contact with this blood. In the case of sex, as we have discussed, anytime fluids are shared, the chance of becoming infected exists.

From Mother to Child

An unborn fetus within a woman who is HIV-positive also has a high chance of becoming infected with HIV. In fact, mother-to-child transmission, called vertical transmission, has resulted in 90 percent of infant and childhood infections worldwide. Though in this book the specifics of how this occurs will not be discussed, generally, transmission occurs as a result of the baby's continuous contact with and reliance upon the mother's infected blood and fluids while in the womb.

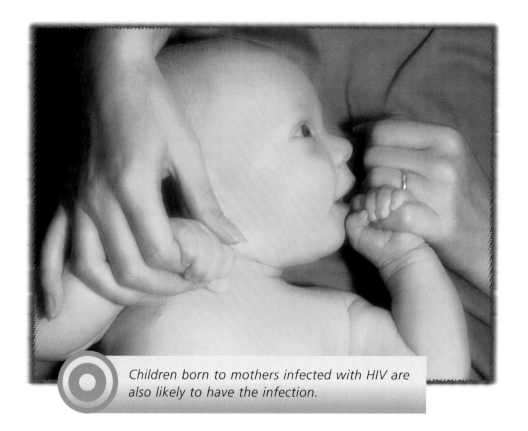

Children born to mothers infected with HIV are also likely to have the infection.

High-Risk Behaviors

Your teen years are often a time of exploration. You engage new friends, experiences, and ideas in the hope of discovering more about yourself. In so doing, you may go to parties, date people, and hang out with your friends. As part of the learning and growing process, you may make decisions that are not the best for you. Unfortunately, sometimes these decisions can impact your life in dramatic ways.

None of this information is meant to scare you into making good decisions. Instead, you are being provided with these facts so that you may know the

Becoming Infected

- You cannot get AIDS from a toilet seat.

- Touching a doorknob that has been touched by a person with HIV will not infect you.

- Bites from bugs, such as mosquitoes, cannot transmit the virus.

- Swimming in a pool with an infected person will not give you the disease.

- Working with or being friends with a person who has HIV will not infect you.

- You will not get AIDS from giving blood.

- Sharing saliva, when kissing someone or sharing a straw, for example, will not infect you.

- You can become infected from sharing a needle when injecting intravenous drugs.

- You may contract the virus if you have unprotected sex with a person who has HIV.

- Coming in contact with the blood of someone who has the virus puts you at risk.

possible consequences of your actions and not have to learn the hard way after the fact. Many teens do not believe that becoming HIV positive can happen to them, until it does.

Drugs and Alcohol

A recent study of the link between teen alcohol consumption and sexual practices established that drinking increases the chances that teens will not use a condom during sex. Whether you forget or you are too drunk or high to care, HIV infection is a real possibility. In terms of drugs, especially intravenous ones, the risk is even greater. Keep in mind that intravenous drug use is one of the three main ways that people contract HIV. Furthermore, drug use has many other negative effects, such as addiction and immediate death. If you are using intravenous drugs, please seek help.

Women and Girls

◎ Young women are the fastest growing group that is contracting HIV/AIDS through unprotected sex.

◎ AIDS is the fourth leading cause of death among women between the ages of twenty-five and forty-four. (Most were infected as teens.)

◎ African American and Hispanic women make up 75 percent of HIV/AIDS cases, yet they account for only 21 percent of the population.

◎ Worldwide, more than 75 percent of all HIV cases have resulted from hetero-sexual intercourse.

◎ Approximately 41 percent of the popula-tion of HIV-infected people are women.

Now that you know how the virus is contracted and how to protect yourself from it, the next chapter will discuss the symptoms of AIDS and HIV testing.

Chapter 3

Getting Tested

For a while now, Chris had not been feeling like himself. It was strange—he was tired, and recently, he had noticed that he was losing weight. He talked to his girlfriend Sarah about it and she said she too had been feeling a bit down. She suggested that maybe they were passing it back and forth or something.

Chris decided to see what his parents thought, so one night after dinner he sat down and told them what was going on.

"You guys, I haven't been feeling like myself lately and I think I might be sick. Mom, do you think that you can make an appointment with Dr. Green, so he can check me out?"

"Sure, honey. Do you have any idea what it is?"

"Um, I don't know. But I know that Sarah has been feeling the same way. She thinks we might be passing it back and forth or something."

"Have you guys been having sex?" asked his dad.

"Well, yeah. But we've been really careful. Sarah's on the pill so she won't get pregnant."

"Chris," said his father, "I'm going to call the doctor tomorrow and make an appointment. I'll call the school and tell them to let you know what time I'll pick you up."

"Dad, I can drive myself. I'm not that sick."

"No, I'm taking you."

The next day on the way to the doctor's office, Chris and his father were quiet almost the whole time.

"Dad, do you think it's cancer?"

"No, Chris. I don't. Let's just see what the doctor says, OK?"

A week later during dinner the phone rang. "Chris," his mother called, "It's Dr. Green. He wants to know if you can come in tomorrow morning for the test results."

"He'll be there," answered his dad. "Just tell him we'll all be there."

When his mom came back to the table, Chris's dad started crying.

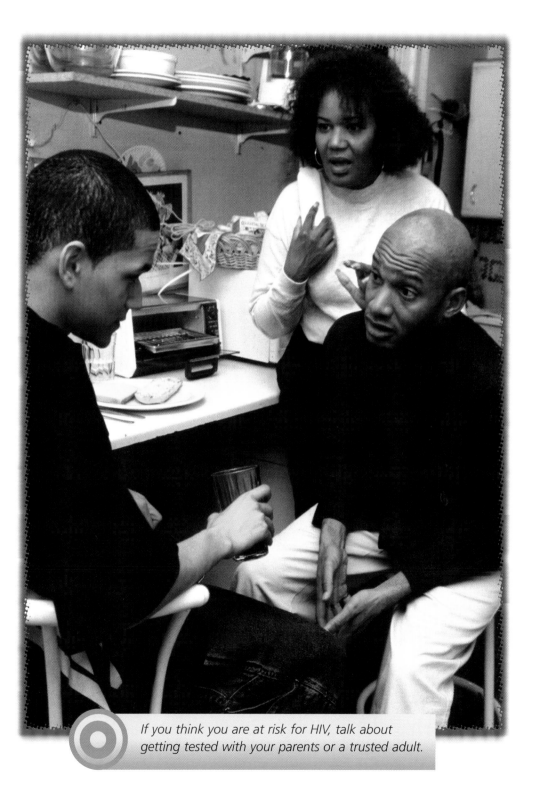

If you think you are at risk for HIV, talk about getting tested with your parents or a trusted adult.

"Chris, I wanted to wait and have Dr. Green tell us in his office tomorrow, but I talked to Dr. Green earlier this afternoon. I asked him to call me as soon as he found something out."

"So, what's wrong with me then? Do I have some weird disease or something?" Chris asked half-jokingly.

"No, Chris, you're HIV positive. I'm sorry but I think Sarah is, too."

HIV Symptoms

HIV is rarely diagnosed right after infection, meaning that years usually pass before a person decides to be tested for the virus, usually because they start to experience some symptoms. This late diagnosis is common because the onset of symptoms varies greatly from person to person. Also, the symptoms of HIV that you will read about in the list below may be mistaken for the signs of many other illnesses, such as the flu or mononucleosis. This is precisely why doctors stress that anyone who has participated in high-risk behavior be tested. Symptoms of HIV infection include the following:

◎ **Prolonged fever**

◎ **Diarrhea**

◎ **Loss of 10 percent or more of your body weight**

- Night sweats

- Persistently swollen glands, especially in the neck, armpits, or groin

- Change in mental behavior such as being forgetful or confused

Testing

As you can see from the list above, the symptoms of HIV are not terribly obvious. They do resemble, or look like, those of many other illnesses. Therefore, if you are experiencing any of the symptoms on the list it does not necessarily mean that you have HIV, nor does it mean that you do not. What it does mean is that you need to be tested. Remember, though, that there are other reasons why you should be tested for HIV. Waiting until you experience symptoms is one of the worst things that you can do. You might unknowingly infect other people, and you could miss out on treatments that can help you if you are infected. So—how do you know if you need to be tested?

Doctors recommend that anyone who has put him or herself at risk should be tested. That means if you have had sex without a condom, get tested, not only for your safety, but for the safety of others. If you can answer yes to any of the following questions, you should schedule an HIV test.

◎ Have you had unprotected sex, sex without a condom?

◎ Are you pregnant? Are you planning on becoming pregnant?

◎ Do you have a sexually transmitted disease or have you been sexually abused?

◎ Have you had sex with someone who has ever injected drugs using a needle?

◎ Do you have tuberculosis?

◎ Did you receive a blood transfusion between early 1978 and mid-1985?

The Tests

HIV tests are actually very simple procedures. A physician, nurse, or clinic worker merely draws blood from your arm using a sterilized syringe. This process usually takes only a few minutes. Your blood is then shipped off to a laboratory to be tested for the HIV virus. Your results will be available to you anywhere from a week to three weeks later. There are, however, different places that you can go to get tested, and different types of tests.

Types of Testing

Today, if you want an HIV test you have several choices. First, decide where you want to be tested.

There are a lot of resources out there. Hospitals, private doctors, family planning or sexually transmitted disease clinics, mobile sites, health departments, and even many Web sites offer HIV testing. Some are free, while others will cost money.

Most important, keep in mind that making a decision like this is not an easy one, and educating yourself will help you make the best decision about what test is right for you. Please check out the list of resources in the Where to Go for Help section at the back of this book to read even more about HIV testing. These organizations can direct you to resources that are available in your community. Once you have decided where you want to be tested, the next step is to choose the type of test you want. Currently, there are two types of tests that you can choose from—anonymous HIV testing and confidential HIV testing.

Anonymous HIV Testing

Taking an anonymous HIV test means that you do not give your name. Instead, you will be given a unique code that identifies you. You will be the only person who knows your test results. This type of test is available in most states.

At-home tests, also known as collection kits, are also anonymous. You can order this test over the phone or online, and then have it shipped to you. You are also the person who administers the test. You take a sample of your blood and send it out to a laboratory. In a few weeks, you learn the results. Again, the results are not given to anyone and most are considered to be quite accurate.

Confidential HIV Testing

Unlike the anonymous HIV testing, confidential HIV testing—also called names testing—does release your name to the health department and medical personnel. Also, if you choose, you can have the results added to your medical record, so doctors know of your status. This type of testing is available in all states.

Regardless of which test you choose, one of the most important things to remember is that the decision to be tested is a smart, healthy one. Getting an HIV test if you have participated in high-risk behavior is a way of taking control of your life and of asserting responsibility for your actions. Though facing the potential consequences can be scary, it is best to know and to live proactively.

Talk to Someone

Waiting for the results of your test can feel like you are waiting to hear the outcome of the rest of your life. Two weeks can feel like an eternity and you may have

AIDS Around the World

The United States is not the only country dealing with the AIDS crisis. Indeed, this terrifying disease affects every country in the world. In Africa, the scope of the AIDS epidemic is tremendous. Though new infections in the year 2000 totaled 3.8 million, this number was down from the 4 million that became infected in 1999.

Nevertheless, this is still an alarming number of people who are becoming infected each year. In 2000, the number of people living with HIV or AIDS in Africa and the Middle East was 25.7 million. In Asia, 6.4 million people were living with HIV or AIDS, and in Latin America and the Caribbean, there were 1.7 million cases. In total, at the end of 2000, 36.1 million people around the world were living with HIV or AIDS.

many serious and confusing thoughts. Talking to someone about how you feel is crucial. A lot of the places that offer testing also offer free counseling. There you can share your feelings of fear, remorse, anger, and pain. You may also rely on a close friend or a parent to help you through this time.

After you receive your results, you should see a counselor one more time. Obviously, if the results come back positive you will be moving into a challenging period of your life. Having someone to talk to can help you cope with the news. But even if the results are negative it is good to talk through your feelings. While negative test results can most certainly bring relief, most health-care workers hope they will not see you again. They hope that you will take precautions and modify any high-risk behaviors.

But what if your results are positive? You might feel as though your life has just been turned upside down and all that you hoped for has come to a screeching halt. Such feelings are very normal. You will have to consider telling your family, as well as finding the right doctor, types of treatment, and most important, how to go on living your life.

Chris's Story

It has been four months now, and Chris still doesn't know how he feels. He has stopped attending school and has pretty much just

If your HIV test result is positive, you might think about sharing your feelings with a counselor.

stopped attending life. He and Sarah broke up because they constantly reminded each other of their shared illness. So Chris just sits at home all day thinking about how he is going to die.

One day as Chris sat staring at the television, his dad walked into the living room.

"Aren't you supposed to be at work?" said Chris.

"Yes, but I came home to talk to you. Your mom and I are incredibly worried. We know this is the hardest thing that has ever happened to you, to us. And we want to support you. We have given you these past couple of months to mourn, and now it is time for you to live again.

Chris, you are still alive. You need to live. Tonight we're all going to a support group for people who are living with AIDS. Living, Chris, not dying."

"I know you're right, Dad. I think about it all the time. I am still alive, but what's the point? I'm going to die."

"Chris, we all are. You just know what you will probably die from."

Chapter 4

Living with HIV and AIDS

If you or someone you know has recently been diagnosed HIV positive, this is undoubtedly an emotional time. You, your friend, or family member may feel scared, angry, out of control, and shocked. You might even be in denial and try to forget the outcome of the test. This is all very common for someone dealing with being HIV positive—this stage is something anyone might go through. Finding out something like this takes time to digest. It is difficult and challenging. Maybe words do not offer much comfort right now. But then what does?

The Centers for Disease Control and Prevention has published a document for people who are living with AIDS. In this document, people infected with HIV share their reactions to and express their feelings about their status. In each one of their statements they describe how hard it was to accept their illness. But they also express how taking control of their lives and treatment turned out to be one of the best ways to deal with the diagnosis. They took control of their illness by not letting it take control of them.

When Chris entered the YMCA room with his parents he felt really uncomfortable at first. But soon afterward, a young woman came over and introduced herself.

"Hi. My name's Adriana. What's yours?"

"I'm Chris, and these are my parents, Cindy and Tom. Come here often?"

"Every Wednesday," said Adriana with a smile. "Is this your first time?"

"Yeah, I'm pretty nervous."

"Really? Come sit by me then, cause I feel like I'm a pro at this by now. The meeting's about to start."

After the session, Chris and Adriana walked out together. Chris let out a long sigh.

"It's amazing, huh?" asked Adriana.

"What do you mean?"

"That we can all be so different but be feeling the same things. It makes you feel sane, less alone in your fight."

"Yeah," said Chris. "Thanks for introducing yourself to me tonight."

"No problem," said Adriana. "How long have you known?"

"Four months."

"It gets better and worse, I promise," said Adriana with a smile.

Support Groups and Caregivers

Joining support groups, talking with counselors, and seeking out caregivers are all highly recommended ways of helping yourself cope with HIV and AIDS. These people offer you emotional support and help you better understand treatment methods. They also teach you how to adjust your lifestyle so you will be more able to fight HIV infection and the disease known as AIDS.

Support groups are a way to meet people who share similar emotions and experiences, and they can also offer you an enormous amount of comfort. Just knowing that other people are out there with you, fighting just the way you are, will take away some of the isolation you may be experiencing. Or perhaps you are feeling isolated and alone because you have not told your family. Maybe you are too scared or just not ready to share. Whatever your reasons for silence are now, at some point in the near future you will probably want to tell your friends and family about your HIV infection. And when you do, you will want to be prepared.

Hospice

People living with AIDS often rely on hospice organizations. A hospice is not a shelter, or even really a place, but rather a group of people confronting terminal illnesses such as AIDS who want to feel in control of their lives and their treatment. The word *hospice* actually stems from the Latin word *hospitium* meaning "guesthouse." Originally, the term referred to a place of shelter for people who were returning from religious pilgrimages and had fallen ill. The first hospice in the United States was established in New Haven, Connecticut, in 1974.

Hospice doctors, registered nurses, counselors, and social workers work with a patient and the patient's doctor to help plan treatments and manage pain—providing advice and support all the while. Eighty percent of their services are offered at the patient's home. Today, there are more than 3,100 hospice programs in the United States, and they provide care for more than 540,000 people.

Anna had been friends with Chris for six months before he told her. She can still remember the fear on his face. He had asked to meet her after school, in a coffee shop downtown. It was the same place they had met.

"Anna, I have something to tell you. It's really serious, and I'm sorry that I didn't tell you before. I was just scared that you wouldn't want to hang out anymore, and I love our relationship so much. You're one of my best friends."

"Chris, what is it? You can tell me anything."

"Anna, I'm HIV positive."

Anna didn't know what to say. Of course she knew about AIDS. Who didn't? But Chris, one of her favorite people in the world, HIV positive! "Oh my god, when? How?"

"I found out two years ago. I was only sixteen, and that's why I took off school for a year. It was really hard, because I got it from my ex-girlfriend, Sarah. She had no idea that she was positive. So when I told her, it was like I was telling her she would die, that we both would."

"Oh, Chris, I'm so sorry and I'm so glad that you shared this with me. This must be tough for you. Thank you for trusting me."

"So you're not scared that I'll infect you? You still want to be my friend?"

"Of course I do, though I definitely think I need to read up on it, and if you don't mind, I would like you to tell me about it some more. But no, I'm not scared."

Telling Your Family and Friends

There is no easy way to tell the people you love that you are HIV positive. However, there are ways for you to be prepared—to make it easier for you and them. The first thing to do is to think about why you are going to tell them. It may seem like an obvious answer: They should know. But take time to think about the various reactions they might have. Is there a particular reaction you hope they have? Do you want them to be supportive of you and learn with you as you educate yourself about the disease? Do you want them to come to the doctor's office, or would you rather go alone and tell them about it later? What will you do if their reaction is not the one you want it to be?

All of these questions allow you to explore your emotions in advance of what will probably be a highly emotional and very important conversation. It helps, too, if you bring along materials—pamphlets, books, brochures—about HIV and AIDS to give to the people in your life so they too can learn about the disease. This also demonstrates that you would like them to try to understand and accept your illness.

Before discussing your HIV positive status with family and friends, you may want to consider how and where you would like that conversation to happen.

You might also consider the environment in which you share this news with your friends and family. Would you rather tell everyone individually, in small groups, or all together? This is your decision, and you must think about what would make you feel most at ease and least overwhelmed. If some of these decisions are too hard for you right now, enlist the help of a friend who knows what's going on or the help of a counselor. Again, please see the Where to Go For Help section in the back of this book if you need advice or informational brochures about HIV and AIDS.

Be patient with your family and friends and give them time to sort out their feelings regarding your HIV status.

Finally, remember to be optimistic about their reactions, but also keep in mind that it might take some time for the shock to wear off. Remember how hard it was for you to digest the news? It will be hard for your friends and family, too. Something that may put all of you at ease is finding the right doctor or medical treatment.

Finding the Right Doctor

In addition to finding a counselor or support system, it is important to find a doctor you can trust. Peace of mind will come from knowing that your doctor not only has your best interests in mind, but that he or she can

How to Protect Others

Knowing that you are HIV positive puts a whole new spin on relationships. Not only must you be careful not to infect the other person but you may fear telling a person you care for that you are HIV positive. As hard as it may be to chance rejection, being open and honest about your HIV status is the most responsible thing for you to do. The list below points out a few things you can do to protect the people in your life.

Do not have unprotected sex.

Do tell your partner that you are HIV positive. He or she has a right to know.

Tell people with whom you have had sex that you have been diagnosed with HIV.

Do not share your toothbrush or razor with others.

If you are thinking about having a child or if you become pregnant, talk to your doctor right away.

If you have a drug abuse problem, do not share needles, and be sure to also seek help for your addiction.

communicate them to you. Your doctor will be able to explain your treatment, what you will experience, and how you might feel.

Finding the right doctor might take a while, but in this case it is in your best interest to be choosy. Meet with different doctors, ask them how they approach the disease and its treatment, and then decide which one seems to be the best. This is also why telling your family and friends might be a good idea. They can help you figure out what to look for in a doctor.

What can you expect from treatment? Is it a lengthy process? Will you need to visit the hospital every day? Knowing some basics about treatment methods will help prepare you for seeing a doctor and enable you to make a more informed decision.

Treatment

Treatment for HIV and AIDS is different for everybody. The infection and disease progress differently from person to person. After many tests and discussions, your doctor will design a medical plan that is right for you. In most cases, especially in the initial stages, you can take pills at home and visit the doctor a few times a week.

Drug Treatments

Researchers have developed many drugs to treat HIV and AIDS, all used in combination with one another. Most often, patients will be given a combination of nucleoside analogs, protease inhibitors, and non-nucleoside reverse transcriptase inhibitors. Basically, each one of these medications keeps your immune system strong by protecting your T-helper cells, thereby keeping your T-helper cell count above 200. Your doctor might prescribe AZT, Videx, Zerit, Epivir (nucleoside analogs); Invirase, Fortovase, Norvir (protease inhibitors); and Rescriptor and Viramune (non-nucleoside reverse transcriptase inhibitors). These drugs are incredibly powerful, and you must follow your doctor's instructions faithfully.

Because many HIV-positive patients can become sick from illnesses a healthy body might normally fight off, doctors often prescribe other medications. This is why it is important to inform your doctor of changes in how you feel. If you encounter any of the trouble-signs listed below, consult your doctor immediately.

◎ **Breathing problems**

◎ **Mouth problems, like white spots or trouble swallowing**

◎ **Fever for more than two days**

◎ **Weight loss**

◎ **Poor vision**

◎ **Diarrhea**

◎ **Skin rashes or itching**

One of the most important things that you must do for yourself is to follow your doctor's advice and keep your doctor's appointments. If you want to take care of yourself and be as healthy as you can be, adhering to your treatment plan is a must. There are, however, other things that you can do to care for yourself.

Taking Charge of Your Health

While taking care of your health by exercising and eating right is important even when you are healthy, when you are sick it is even more vital. People who have HIV and AIDS have weak immune systems, so their bodies have a more difficult time battling the bacteria found in foods. If you eat healthy foods, you will increase your energy level and strength; your body will be better able to protect itself. However, it is also important that you rest and relax. Knowing you are sick can increase your stress level. Many people with HIV practice meditation in an effort to relieve stress.

Finally, if you're not HIV positive, immunizations are also a great way to keep your body healthy. Immunizations are shots of small doses of an illness such as the flu or pneumonia. Immunizations allow your body to build up antibodies to the sickness, so it will become better equipped to destroy it. For further information, ask your doctor about these shots.

It is important to maintain your health. Practicing yoga and meditation are good ways to positively affect both your body and mind.

Future of HIV and AIDS

Unfortunately, HIV and AIDS are not nearing extinction. In fact, researchers do not believe that a cure for the disease will be found soon. Each time researchers think they are close, the virus mutates, or adjusts in order to thrive. Still, with new treatments, people do have a chance to live full lives even though they have the HIV virus, and with more education, it is hoped that people will protect themselves from the disease. If people learn what to do to prevent HIV infection, they won't have to learn how to live with it.

Glossary

AIDS Disease that is caused by the HIV virus; diagnosed once a person's T-helper cell count drops below 200; aquired immunodeficiency syndrome.

anonymous HIV testing Type of HIV testing in which the person tested is given a unique code, rather than using his or her name; the test is completely confidential.

cell count Test that is done to count the number of T-cells left in an HIV or AIDS patient's immune system.

confidential HIV testing Type of HIV test that uses your name and releases it to medical personnel; also called names testing.

GRID Early term used for AIDS; stands for gay-related immune deficiency.

hemophilia   Condition in which a person's blood does not clot properly; causes excessive bleeding from a slight injury.

HIV   Virus that causes AIDS; stands for human immunodeficiency virus.

immune system   System of the body that fights off illness; the system that the HIV virus attacks and weakens.

intravenous drug use   Directly injecting drugs into the bloodstream using a needle.

Kaposi's sarcoma   Type of cancer that initially triggered researchers to study the condition that came to be known as AIDS.

safe sex   General term used to describe sex that does not permit infections and illnesses to pass from one person to another; most often related to the use of a condom.

T-helper cell   Type of white blood cell that helps fight off bacteria and viruses that enter the body; cell that the HIV virus attacks and destroys.

vertical transmission   Term used to describe how the HIV virus is passed from mother to unborn child.

white blood cells   Cells that circulate in the blood and lymphatic system; part of the immune system responsible for attacking foreign invasions of the body.

Where to Go for Help

In the United States

AIDS Treatment Data Network
611 Broadway, Suite 613
New York, NY 10012
(800) 734-7104
Web site: http://www.aidsinfonyc.org/network

Centers for Disease Control and Prevention
1600 Clifton Road
Atlanta, GA 30333
(800) 311-3435
Web site: http://www.cdc.gov

HIV/AIDS Treatment Information Service
P.O. Box 6303

Rockville, MD 20849-6303
(800) HIV-0440 (448-0440)
Web site: http://www.hivatis.org

Hospice Foundation of America
2001 S Street NW, Suite 300
Washington, DC 20009
(800) 854-3402
Web site: http://www.hospicefoundation.org

National Association of People with AIDS
1413 K Street NW, Seventh Floor
Washington, DC 20005
(202) 898-0414
Web site: http://www.napwa.org

National Prevention Information Network
P.O. Box 6003
Rockville, MD 20849-6003
(800) 458-5231
Web site: http://www.cdcnpin.org

Project Inform
205 13th Street, #2001
San Francisco, CA 94103
(800) 822-7422
Web site: http://www.projinf.org

The Body
250 West 57th Street
New York, NY 10019.
Web site: http://www.thebody.com

In Canada

AIDS Foundation of Canada
885 Dunsmuir Street, Suite 1000
Vancouver, BC V6C 2T6
(604) 688 7294
Web site: http://www.aidsfoundation.ca

Canadian AIDS Society
130 Albert Street, Suite 900
Ottawa, ON K1P 5G4
(613) 230-3580
Web site: http://www.cdnaids.ca

Canadian HIV/AIDS Clearinghouse
1565 Carling Avenue, Suite 400
Ottawa, ON K1Z 8R1
(613) 725-3434
Web site: http://www.clearinghouse.cpha.ca

For Further Reading

Ford, Michael Thomas. *100 Questions and Answers About AIDS: A Guide for Young People.* New York: New Discovery Books, 1992.

Ford, Michael Thomas. *The Voices of AIDS: Twelve Unforgettable People Talk About How AIDS Has Changed Their Lives.* New York: Morrow Junior Books, 1995.

Gonzales, Doreen. *AIDS: Ten Stories of Courage.* Springfield, NJ: Enslow Publishers, 1996.

Manning, Karen. *AIDS: Can This Epidemic Be Stopped.* New York: Twenty-First Century Books, 1995.

Martelli, Leonard J. *When Someone You Know Has AIDS: A Practical Guide.* Rev. Ed. New York: Crown Trade Paperbacks, 1993.

Roleff, Tamara L., and Charles P. Cozic, eds. *AIDS: Opposing Viewpoints.* San Diego: Greenhaven Press, 1998.

Silverstein, Alvin, Virginia B. Silverstein, Laura Silverstein Nunn. *AIDS: An All-About Guide for Young Adults.* Springfield, NJ: Enslow Publishers, 1999.

Storad, Conrad J. *Inside AIDS: HIV Attacks the Immune System.* Minneapolis, MN: Lerner Publications Co., 1998.

Index

A

abstinence, 22
AIDS
  discovery of, 8–12
  future of, 54
  living with, 41–54
  myths about, 19, 26
  origins of, 14
  statistics on, 10–11, 12, 18, 27–28
  timeline of, 10–11
  treatment for, 11, 38, 42, 43, 44,
    50–52, 54
  in United States, 7, 10, 12, 37
  what it is, 18
  worldwide, 7, 37
alcohol, 27
anonymous HIV testing, 35–36
at-home tests, 35
AZT, 11, 51

B

bacteria, 14, 52
blood, 9, 12, 20, 24, 26, 34, 36
  contact with, 11, 12, 20, 23, 26
  transfusion, 9, 12, 34

C

cancer, 8, 17
caregivers, 43
Centers for Disease Control and
    Protection (CDC), 8, 9, 41
clinics, 35
condoms, 20, 23, 24, 27, 33, 34
confidential HIV testing, 35, 36
counselor/counseling, 38, 43, 44, 47, 48

D

doctor, finding the right, 48–50
drugs, 9, 24, 26, 27, 34, 49
drug treatments, 50–51

E

education about HIV/AIDS,
    importance of, 7, 35, 46, 54

F

family and friends, telling about
    being HIV positive, 38, 43,
    46–48, 49, 50
feelings, dealing with your, 38, 41,
    43, 46

Food and Drug Administration (FDA), 11

G
GRID (gay-related immune deficiency), 8, 10

H
health department, 35, 36
hemophilia, 9, 12
high-risk behavior, 25–27, 32, 36, 38
HIV
    contracting, 11, 12, 19–27
    discovery of, 10–12, 24
    future of, 54
    living with, 41–54
    myths about, 26
    statistics on, 6, 10–11, 12, 24, 27–28, 37
    symptoms of, 32–33
    testing for, 11–12, 32, 33–36, 38
    what it is, 14
homosexuality, 8, 9, 20
hospice, 44

I
immune system, 7, 8, 9, 14–17, 18, 51, 52
immunizations, 52
infections, 8, 9, 14, 17
Institut Pasteur, 10
intravenous drug use, 9, 24, 26, 27, 34

K
Kaposi's sarcoma, 8

L
lung disease, 17

M
mother to unborn child transmission/vertical transmission, 20, 24

O
oral sex, 22

P
pneumonia, 9, 18, 52
protecting yourself and others from infection, 6–7, 17, 19, 20, 22–23, 24, 49, 54

S
safe sex, 20–23
semen, 11
sexual/bodily fluids, 11, 20, 22, 23
sexual intercourse/contact, 11, 20, 22–23, 24, 26, 27, 33, 49
sharing needles, 9, 24, 26, 49
support groups/system, 43, 48

T
taking control of your life, 42, 44, 52
talking to someone, 36–38, 46
tests for HIV
    reasons to have, 33–34, 36
    types of, 34–36
T-helper cells, 9, 15, 16, 17, 18, 51
tuberculosis, 17, 18, 34

W
women/girls, statistics on, 27–28

About the Author

Katherine White is a freelance writer and editor. She lives in Brooklyn, NY.

Photo Credits

Cover © Maura Boruchow; pp. 2, 21, 22, 31, 39, 47, 48, 53 © Ira Fox; p. 13 © TimePix; pp. 15, 23 © CMSP; p. 25 © John Parnell/Indexstock.